we ac-know-ledge thee,
we ac-know-ledge thee,
we ac-know-ledge thee,
we ac-know-ledge thee,
Reeds
Ped.
thee to be the Lord.
thee to be the Lord.
thee to be the Lord.
thee to be the Lord.
thee to be the Lord.
thee to be the Lord.
ff
All the
All the
All the
Gt. f
Reeds
1

26
S.1
earth doth wor - ship thee:
S.2
earth doth wor - ship thee:
A.
ff
All the earth doth wor - ship thee:
T.1
earth doth wor - ship thee:
T.2
ff
All the earth doth wor - ship thee:
B.
ff
All the earth doth wor - ship thee:
26
Gt. f
Reeds
Ped.
31
S.
the Fa - ther ev - er - last - ing.
A.
the Fa - ther ev - er - last - ing.
T.
the Fa - ther ev - er - last - ing.
B.
the Fa - ther ev - er - last - ing.
31
Gt. +
Reeds
Gt.

38
2
f
To thee all
To thee all
To thee all
To thee all
ff
Reeds
44
An - gels cry a-loud:
An - gels cry a-loud:
An - gels cry a-loud:
An - gels cry a-loud:
Gt.
(Ped.)
(Gt.)
Reeds

49
the Heavens, and all the Powers there-in.
the Heavens, and all the Powers there-in.
the Heavens, and all the Powers there-in.
the Heavens, and all the Powers there-in.
49
Gt.
(Ped.)
55
CHOIR 1
3 più animato (𝅗𝅥. = 58-60)
mp
cresc.
To thee Che-ru-bin, and
To thee Che-ru-bin, and
To thee Che-ru-bin, and
To thee Che-ru-bin, and
55
3 più animato (𝅗𝅥. = 58-60)
Gt.
Sw. fp
cresc.

58
CHOIR 1
Se-ra-phin con-tin-ual-ly do cry,
Se-ra-phin con-tin-ual-ly do cry,
Se-ra-phin con-tin-ual-ly do cry,
Se-ra-phin con-tin-ual-ly do cry,
58
CHOIR 2
mf
cresc.
To thee Che-ru-bin, and Se-ra-phin con - tin-ual - ly do
To thee Che-ru-bin, and Se-ra-phin con - tin-ual - ly do
To thee Che-ru-bin, and Se-ra-phin con - tin-ual - ly do
To thee Che-ru-bin, and Se-ra-phin con - tin-ual - ly do
58
mfp
cresc.

* Whenever possible, this part should be sung by a counter-tenor.

66
SOLI
-ly, Ho-ly, Ho-ly: Lord God_ of Sa-ba-oth;
-ly, Ho-ly, Ho-ly: Lord God_ of Sa-ba-oth;
-ly, Ho-ly, Ho-ly: Lord God_ of Sa-ba-oth;
66
CHOIRS 1 and 2
f
Ho - ly,
f
Ho - ly,
mf
Ho - ly,
mf
Ho - ly,
66
f
mf
(Ped.)
CHOIRS 1 and 2
72
ppp
5
pochiss. allarg.
Ho - ly, Ho-ly, Ho-ly: Lord God_ of Sa-ba-oth;
ppp
Ho - ly, Ho-ly, Ho-ly: Lord God_ of Sa-ba-oth;
ppp
Ho - ly, Ho-ly, Ho-ly: Lord God_ of Sa-ba-oth;
ppp
Ho - ly, Ho-ly, Ho-ly: Lord God_ of Sa-ba-oth;
72
5
pochiss. allarg.
(Gt.) p cresc. molto
+ 32'

CHOIR 1
a tempo animato come prima
S.
Lord God of Sa-ba-oth; Heaven and earth are
A.
Lord God of Sa-ba-oth; Heaven and earth are
T.
Lord God of Sa-ba-oth; Heaven and earth are
B.
Lord God of Sa-ba-oth; Heaven and earth are
CHOIR 2
a tempo animato come prima
S.
Lord God of Sa-ba-oth, Lord God of Sa - ba-oth;
A.
Lord God of Sa-ba-oth, Lord God of Sa - ba-oth;
T.
Lord God of Sa-ba-oth, Lord God of Sa - ba-oth;
B.
Lord God of Sa-ba-oth, Lord God of Sa - ba-oth;
a tempo animato come prima
(Gt.)
Sw.
cresc.
-32′

82
full of the Ma - jes - ty of thy glo - ry,
full of the Ma - jes - ty of thy glo - ry,
full of the Ma - jes - ty of thy glo - ry,
full of the Ma - jes - ty of thy glo - ry,
82
f
Heaven and earth are
Heaven and earth are
Heaven and earth are
Heaven and earth are
82
f mf cresc.

84
Heaven and earth are
Heaven and earth are
Heaven and earth are
Heaven and earth are
84
full of the Ma - jes - ty of thy glo - ry,
full of the Ma - jes - ty of thy glo - ry,
full of the Ma - jes - ty of thy glo - ry,
full of the Ma - jes - ty of thy glo - ry,
84
f mf cresc.

86
ff
full of the Ma - jes - ty of thy glo - ry,
full of the Ma - jes - ty of thy glo - ry,
full of the Ma - jes - ty of thy glo - ry.
full of the Ma - jes - ty of thy glo - ry.
of the Ma - jes - ty of thy glo - ry,
of the Ma - jes - ty of thy glo - ry.
of the Ma - jes - ty of thy glo - ry.
of the Ma - jes - ty of thy glo - ry.
(Gt.)
8va
(Gt.) ff dim. f
mf
+ 32′

* Whenever possible, these parts should be sung by boys only.

98
thee.
thee.
The goodly fellowship of the Prophets
The goodly fellowship of the Prophets
98
pp
Ped.
101
p
praise thee.
praise thee.
praise thee.
praise thee. The
praise thee. The
praise thee. The
101
pp legato
Man.

105
praise
praise
1.
2.
noble army of Martyrs praise thee.
praise
noble army of Martyrs praise thee.
noble army of Martyrs praise thee.
105
pp
Ped.
Man.
108
7
poco stringendo
pp
cresc.
thee.
through-out all the
thee.
The holy Church through-out all the
thee.
The holy Church through-out all the
The holy Church through-out all the
The holy Church through-out all the
108
7
poco stringendo
(Man.)

112
pochiss. allarg.
world doth ac - know-ledge thee: the Fa - ther of an in - fi - nite
world doth ac - know-ledge thee: the Fa - ther of an in - fi - nite
world doth ac - know-ledge thee: the Fa - ther of an in - fi - nite
world doth ac - know-ledge thee: the Fa - ther of an in - fi - nite
112
pochiss. allarg.
Gt. f
Ped.
116
a tempo
Ma - jes - ty;
Ma - jes - ty;
Ma - jes - ty; Thine hon-our - a - ble,
Ma - jes - ty; Thine hon-our - a - ble,
a tempo
116
ff dim.
mf
dim.
pp

120
p
3
Al-so the Ho - ly Ghost the
p
3
Al-so the Ho - ly Ghost the
true, and on - ly Son;
true, and on - ly Son;
120
8va
3
Sw. p
3
Man.
123
poco rit.
Com-fort-er.
Com-fort-er.
pp
3
Al-so the Ho - ly Ghost the Com - fort - er.
pp
3
Al-so the Ho - ly Ghost the Com - fort - er.
(8va)
123
(Ch.)
poco rit.
Ch.
pp
Ped.
+32′

126
8 Vivo (♩ = 120-126)
Reeds f
Man.
129
132
Reeds
Gt.
Reeds
(Man.)
135
poco allarg.
ff
Full org. fff
Ped.
G.P.

141
9 Risoluto (poco meno mosso: ♩ = c.116)
fff
S.
Thou art the King of Glo - ry, O Christ. Thou
A.
Thou art the King of Glo - ry, O Christ. Thou
T.
Thou art the King of Glo - ry, O Christ. Thou
B.
Thou art the King of Glo - ry, O Christ. Thou
141
9 Risoluto (poco meno mosso: ♩ = c.116)
Gt. ff
Reeds
Ped.
-32′
144
sub. a tempo vivo (♩ = c.126)
art the ev - er - last - ing Son of the Fa -
art the ev - er - last - ing Son of the Fa -
art the ev - er - last - ing Son of the Fa -
art the ev - er - last - ing Son of the Fa -
sub. a tempo vivo (♩ = c.126)
144
(Gt.)
Sw.
ff
f
Gt.
f

147
ther.
ther.
ther.
ther.
147
149
dim.
pp

153
10
tranquillo (♩ = 84-88)
S.
A.
T.
B.
p
thou
p
thou
p
When thou took-est up-on thee to de-liv - er man:
p
When thou took-est up-on thee to de-liv - er man:
Sw. p
p legato
+32′
-32′
156
poco più lento
didst not ab-hor the Vir - gin's womb.
didst not ab-hor the Vir - gin's womb.
p
When
p
When
8va
Ch.

158
p
thou didst
p
thou didst
thou hadst o - ver - come the sharp - ness of death, thou didst
thou hadst o - ver - come the sharp - ness of death,
158
(Ch.)
p esp.
160
a tempo
più vivace
(♩ = 104-108)
o - pen the king - dom of heaven to all be - liev - ers. Thou
o - pen the king - dom of heaven to all be - liev - ers. Thou
o - pen the king - dom of heaven to all be - liev - ers. Thou
Thou
a tempo
più vivace
(♩ = 104-108)
160
(Ch.)
Gt.
Gt. legato
(Ped.)

163
11
sit - test at the right hand of God: in the glo -
sit - test at the right hand of God: in the glo -
sit - test at the right hand of God: in the glo -
sit - test at the right hand of God: in the glo -
163
11
f
166
Maestoso (♩ = 76-80)
- ry of the Fa-ther.
- ry of the Fa-ther.
- ry of the Fa-ther.
ff
We be - lieve that thou shalt
- ry of the Fa-ther.
ff
We be - lieve that thou shalt
166
Maestoso (♩ = 76-80)
f
Man.

170
rall.
12 a tempo (♩= 88-92)
mp
We there-fore pray thee,
mp
We there - fore pray thee,
come to be our Judge. We there - fore pray thee,
mp
come to be our Judge.
170
rall.
12 a tempo (♩= 88-92)
mp
Ped. sfz
+32′
-32′
173
help thy ser - vants, whom thou hast re - deemed with thy pre - cious blood.
help thy ser - vants, whom thou hast re - deemed with thy pre - cious blood.
help thy ser - vants, whom thou hast re - deemed with thy pre - cious blood.
173

poco stringendo
Make them to be num - bered with thy Saints in
Make them to be num - bered with thy Saints in
Make them to be num - bered with thy Saints
Make them to be num - bered with thy Saints in
poco stringendo
cresc.
legato
ben tenuto
sub. a tempo I (♩= 168-176)
glo - ry ev - er - last - ing.
glo - ry ev - er - last - ing.
in glo - ry ev - er - last - ing.
glo - ry ev - er - last - ing.
sub. a tempo I (♩= 168-176)
Gt. ff

186
ff
Reeds
Gt.
Reeds
191 13
f
O Lord, save thy peo - ple,
O Lord, save thy peo - ple,
O Lord, save thy peo - ple,
O Lord, save thy peo - ple,
191 13
Gt.
(Gt.)

196
and bless thine
and bless thine
and bless thine
and bless thine
(Gt.)
Reeds
Gt.
(Ped.)
201
he - ri-tage. Gov - ern them
he - ri-tage. Gov - ern them
he - ri-tage. Gov - ern them
he - ri-tage. Gov - ern them
(Gt.)
Reeds
Gt.
Reeds

206
CHOIR 1
206
CHOIR 2
and lift them up for
and lift them up for
and lift them up for
and lift them up for
206
Ped.
mf

209 14 animato come prima
f
Day by day we mag - ni - fy thee; And we
Day by day we mag - ni - fy thee; And we
Day by day we mag - ni - fy thee; And we
Day by day we mag - ni - fy thee; And we
209 14 animato come prima
ev - er.
ev - er.
ev - er.
ev - er.
14 animato come prima
209
Gt.
mf
cresc.
Sw.

211
wor - ship thy name,
wor - ship thy name,
wor - ship thy name,
wor - ship thy name,
211
f
Day by day we mag - ni - fy thee; And we
f
Day by day we mag - ni - fy thee; And we
f
Day by day we mag - ni - fy thee; And we
f
Day by day we mag - ni - fy thee; And we
211
f
mf
cresc.

213
pochiss. allarg.
Day by day we mag - ni - fy thee;
Day by day we mag - ni - fy thee;
Day by day we mag - ni - fy thee;
Day by day we mag - ni - fy thee;
pochiss. allarg.
213
ff marcatissimo
wor - ship thy name, And we
ff marcatissimo
wor - ship thy name, And we
ff marcatissimo
wor - ship thy name, And we
ff marcatissimo
wor - ship thy name, And we
pochiss. allarg.
213
f
mf
cresc.
(Gt.)

215
ff marcatissimo
And we wor - ship thy name ev - er
ff marcatissimo
And we wor - ship thy name ev - er
ff marcatissimo
And we wor - ship thy name ev - er
ff marcatissimo
And we wor - ship thy name ev - er
215
wor - ship thy name ev - er
wor - ship thy name ev - er
wor - ship thy name ev - er
wor - ship thy name ev - er
215
f

15 a tempo
217
world with - out end.
world with - out end.
world with - out end.
world with - out end.
15 a tempo
217
world with - out end.
world with - out end.
world with - out end.
world with - out end.
15 a tempo
217
Reeds ff
Gt. ff
ff
+ 32′

*Whenever possible, these parts should be sung by boys only.

232
Vouch - safe, O Lord.
Lord, to keep us this day with - out sin.
Lord, to keep us this day with - out sin.
this day with - out sin.
O
O
O
232
235
O Lord, have mer - cy up -
O Lord, have mer - cy up -
Lord, have mer - cy up - on us, have mer - cy up - on us,
Lord, have mer - cy up - on us, have mer - cy up - on us.
Lord, have mer - cy up - on us, have mer - cy up - on us.
235
pp
legato
Ped.
Man.

238
have mer - cy up - on us. O
- on us, have mer - cy up - on us, have mer - cy up - on us.
- on us, have mer - cy up - on us. O
have mer - cy up - on us.
O
O
O
8va
(rich tone)
Ped. 32′
241 17 più lento (𝅗𝅥 = c.50)
(tutti)
cresc.
Lord, let thy mer - cy light - en up - on us, as our trust is in
poco cresc.

244
ff
thee. O Lord, in thee have I trust -
thee. O Lord, in thee have I trust -
thee. O Lord, in thee have I trust -
thee. O Lord, in thee have I trust -
Gt. f
f
Gt. + sub- and super-octave couplers
Ped.
247
18
marcatiss.
- ed: let me nev - er be con - found - ed,
- ed: let me nev - er be con - found - ed,
- ed: let me nev - er be con - found - ed,
- ed: let me nev - er be con -